The Fish

Alan A. Rubin
Illustrated by Barbara Herzfeld

Rigby®
A Harcourt Achieve Imprint

www.Rigby.com
1-800-531-5015

We were going fishing.
I had to get my pole.

3

We were going fishing.
I had to get my hat.

We were going fishing.
I had to get my net.

We were going fishing.
I had to get my vest.

We were going fishing.
I had to get my boat.

We were going fishing.
I had to get my paddle.

We were going fishing.
I had to get my worm.

I got my fish!